First State of the Union Address

JAMES KNOX POLK

1845

TABLE OF CONTENTS

FELLOW-CITIZENS OF THE SENATE AND OF
THE HOUSE OF REPRESENTATIVES

FELLOW-CITIZENS OF THE SENATE AND OF THE HOUSE OF REPRESENTATIVES

It is to me a source of unaffected satisfaction to meet the representatives of the States and the people in Congress assembled, as it will be to receive the aid of their combined wisdom in the administration of public affairs. In performing for the first time the duty imposed on me by the Constitution of giving to you information of the state of the Union and recommending to your consideration such measures as in my judgment are necessary and expedient, I am happy that I can congratulate you on the continued prosperity of our country. Under the blessings of Divine Providence and the benign influence of our free institutions, it stands before the world a spectacle of national happiness.

With our unexampled advancement in all the elements of national greatness, the affection of the people is confirmed for the Union of the States and for the doctrines of popular liberty which lie at the foundation of our Government.

It becomes us in humility to make our devout acknowledgments to the Supreme Ruler of the Universe for the inestimable civil and religious blessings with which we are favored.

In calling the attention of Congress to our relations with foreign powers, I am gratified to be able to state that though with some of them there have existed since your last session serious causes of irritation and misunderstanding, yet no actual hostilities have taken place. Adopting the maxim in the conduct of our foreign affairs "to ask nothing that is not right and submit to nothing that is wrong," it has been my anxious desire to preserve peace with all nations, but at the same time to be prepared to resist aggression and maintain all our just rights.

In pursuance of the joint resolution of Congress "for annexing Texas to the United States," my predecessor, on the 3d day of March, 1845, elected to submit the first and second sections of that resolution to the Republic of Texas as an overture on the part of the United States for her admission as a State into our Union. This election I approved, and accordingly the charge' d'affaires of the United States in Texas, under instructions of the 10th of March, 1845, presented these sections of the resolution for the acceptance of that Republic. The executive government, the Congress, and the people of Texas in convention have successively complied with all the terms and conditions of the joint resolution. A constitution for the government of the State of Texas, formed by a convention of deputies, is herewith laid before Congress. It is well known, also, that the people of Texas at the polls have accepted the terms of annexation and ratified the constitution. I communicate to Congress the correspondence between the Secretary of State and our charge' d'affaires in Texas, and also the correspondence of the latter with the authorities of Texas, together with the official documents transmitted by him to his own Government. The terms of annexation which were offered by the United States having been accepted by Texas, the public faith of both parties is solemnly pledged to the compact of their union. Nothing remains to consummate the event but the passage of an act by Congress to admit the State of Texas into the Union upon an equal footing with the original States. Strong reasons exist why this should be done at an early period of the session. It will be observed that by the constitution of Texas the existing government is only continued temporarily till Congress can act, and that the third Monday of the present month is the day appointed for holding the first general election. On that day a governor, a lieutenant-governor, and both branches of the legislature will be chosen by the people. The President of Texas is required, immediately after the receipt of official information that the new State has been admitted into our Union by Congress, to convene the legislature, and upon its meeting the existing government will be superseded and the State government organized. Questions deeply interesting to Texas, in common with the other States, the extension of our revenue laws and judicial system over her people and territory, as well as measures of a local character, will claim the early attention of Congress, and therefore upon every principle of republican government she ought to be represented in that body without unnecessary delay. I can not too earnestly recommend prompt action on this important subject. As soon as the act to admit Texas as a State shall be passed the union of the two Republics will be consummated by their own voluntary consent.

This accession to our territory has been a bloodless achievement. No arm of force has been raised to produce the result. The sword has had no part in the victory. We have not sought to extend our territorial possessions by conquest, or our republican institutions over a reluctant people. It was the deliberate homage of each people to the great principle of our federative union. If we consider the extent of territory involved in the annexation, its prospective influence on America, the means by which it has been accomplished, springing purely from the choice of the people themselves to share the blessings of our union, the history of the world may be challenged to furnish a parallel. The jurisdiction of the United States, which at the formation of the Federal Constitution was bounded by the St. Marys on the Atlantic, has passed the capes of Florida and been peacefully extended to the Del Norte. In contemplating the grandeur of this event it is not to be forgotten that the result was achieved in despite of the diplomatic interference of European monarchies. Even France, the country which had been our ancient ally, the country which has a common interest with us in maintaining the freedom of the seas, the country which, by the cession of Louisiana, first opened to us access to the Gulf of Mexico, the country with which we have been every year drawing more and more closely the bonds of successful commerce, most unexpectedly, and to our unfeigned regret, took part in an effort to prevent annexation and to impose on Texas, as a condition of the recognition of her independence by Mexico, that she would never join herself to the United States. We may rejoice that the tranquil and pervading influence of the American principle of self-government was sufficient to defeat the purposes of British and French interference, and that the almost unanimous voice of the people of Texas has given to that interference a peaceful and effective rebuke. From this example European Governments may learn how vain diplomatic arts and intrigues must ever prove upon this continent against that system of self-government which seems natural to our soil, and which will ever resist foreign interference.

Toward Texas I do not doubt that a liberal and generous spirit will actuate Congress in all that concerns her interests and prosperity, and that she will never have cause to regret that she has united her "lone star" to our glorious constellation.

I regret to inform you that our relations with Mexico since your last session have not been of the amicable character which it is our desire to cultivate with all foreign nations. On the 6th day of March last the Mexican envoy extraordinary and minister plenipotentiary to the United States made a formal protest in the name of his Government against the joint resolution passed by Congress "for the annexation of Texas to the United States," which he chose to regard as a violation of the rights of Mexico, and in consequence of it he demanded his passports. He was informed that the Government of the United States did not consider this joint resolution as a violation of any of the rights of Mexico, or that it afforded any just cause of offense to his Government; that the Republic of Texas was an independent power, owing no allegiance to Mexico and constituting no part of her territory or rightful sovereignty and jurisdiction. He was also assured that it was the sincere desire of this Government to maintain with that of Mexico relations of peace and good understanding. That functionary, however, notwithstanding these representations and assurances, abruptly terminated his mission and shortly afterwards left the country. Our envoy extraordinary and minister plenipotentiary to Mexico was refused all official intercourse with that Government, and, after remaining several months, by the permission of his own Government he returned to the United States. Thus, by the acts of Mexico, all diplomatic intercourse between the two countries was suspended.

Since that time Mexico has until recently occupied an attitude of hostility toward the United States-has been marshaling and organizing armies, issuing proclamations, and avowing the intention to make war on the United States, either by an open declaration or by invading Texas. Both the Congress and convention of the people of Texas invited this Government to send an army into that territory to protect and defend them against the menaced attack. The moment the terms of annexation offered by the United States were accepted by Texas the latter became so far a part of our own country as to make it our duty to afford such protection and defense. I therefore deemed it proper, as a precautionary measure, to order a strong squadron to the coasts of Mexico and to concentrate an efficient military force on the western frontier of Texas. Our Army was ordered to take position in the country between the Nueces and the Del Norte, and to repel any invasion of the Texan territory which might be attempted by the Mexican forces. Our squadron in the Gulf was ordered to cooperate with the Army. But though our Army and Navy were placed in a position to defend our own and the rights of Texas, they were ordered to commit no act of hostility against Mexico unless she declared war or was herself the aggressor by striking the first blow. The result has been that Mexico has made no aggressive movement, and our military and naval commanders have executed their orders with such discretion that the peace of the two Republics has not been disturbed. Texas had declared her independence and maintained it by her arms for more than nine years. She has had an organized government in successful operation during that period. Her separate existence as an independent state had been recognized by the United States and the principal powers of Europe. Treaties of commerce and navigation had been concluded with her by different nations, and it had become manifest to the whole world that any further attempt on the part of Mexico to conquer her or overthrow her Government would be vain. Even Mexico herself had become satisfied of this fact, and whilst the question of annexation was pending before the people of Texas during the past summer the Government of Mexico, by a formal act, agreed to recognize the independence of Texas on condition that she would not annex herself to any other power. The agreement to acknowledge the independence of Texas, whether with or without this condition, is conclusive against Mexico. The independence of Texas is a fact conceded by Mexico herself, and she had no right or authority to prescribe restrictions as to the form of government which Texas might afterwards choose to assume. But though Mexico can not complain of the United States on account of the annexation of Texas, it is to be regretted that serious causes of misunderstanding between the two countries continue to exist, growing out of unredressed injuries inflicted by the Mexican authorities and people on the persons and property of citizens of the United States through a long series of years. Mexico has admitted these injuries, but has neglected and refused to repair them. Such was the character of the wrongs and such the insults repeatedly offered to American citizens and the American flag by Mexico, in palpable violation of the laws of nations and the treaty between the two countries of the 5th of April, 1831, that they have been repeatedly brought to the notice of Congress by my predecessors. As early as the 6th of February, 1837, the President of the United States declared in a message to Congress that-

The length of time since some of the injuries have been committed, the repeated and unavailing applications for redress, the wanton character of some of the outrages upon the property and persons of our citizens, upon the officers and flag of the United States, independent of recent insults to this Government and people by the late extraordinary Mexican minister, would justify in the eyes of all nations immediate war.

He did not, however, recommend an immediate resort to this extreme measure, which, he declared, "should not be used by just and generous nations, confiding in their strength for injuries committed, if it can be honorably avoided," but, in a spirit of forbearance, proposed that another demand be made on Mexico for that redress which had been so long and unjustly withheld. In these views committees of the two Houses of Congress, in reports made to their respective bodies, concurred. Since these proceedings more than eight years have elapsed, during which, in addition to the wrongs then complained of, others of an aggravated character have been committed on the persons and property of our citizens. A special agent was sent to Mexico in the summer of 1838 with full authority to make another and final demand for redress. The demand was made; the Mexican Government promised to repair the wrongs of which we complained, and after much delay a treaty of indemnity with that view was concluded between the two powers on the 11th of April, 1839, and was duly ratified by both Governments. By this treaty a joint commission was created to adjudicate and decide on the claims of American citizens on the Government of Mexico. The commission was organized at Washington on the 25th day of August, 1840. Their time was limited to eighteen months, at the expiration of which they had adjudicated and decided claims amounting to $2,026,139.68 in favor of citizens of the United States against the Mexican Government, leaving a large amount of claims undecided. Of the latter the American commissioners had decided in favor of our citizens claims amounting to $928,627.88, which were left unacted on by the umpire authorized by the treaty. Still further claims, amounting to between three and four millions of dollars, were submitted to the board too late to be considered, and were left undisposed of. The sum of $2,026,139.68, decided by the board, was a liquidated and ascertained debt due by Mexico to the claimants, and there was no justifiable reason for delaying its payment according to the terms of the treaty. It was not, however, paid. Mexico applied for further indulgence, and, in that spirit of liberality and forbearance which has ever marked the policy of the United States toward that Republic, the request was granted, and on the 30th of January, 1843, a new treaty was concluded. By this treaty it was provided that the interest due on the awards in favor of claimants under the convention of the 11th of April, 1839, should be paid out the 30th of April, 1843, and that-

The principal of the said awards and the interest accruing thereon shall be paid in five years, in equal installments every three months, the said term of five years to commence on the 30th day of April, 1843, aforesaid.

The interest due on the 30th day of April, 1843, and the three first of the twenty installments have been paid. Seventeen of these installments, remain unpaid, seven of which are now due.

The claims which were left undecided by the joint commission, amounting to more than $3,000,000, together with other claims for spoliations on the property of our citizens, were subsequently presented to the Mexican Government for payment, and were so far recognized that a treaty providing for their examination and settlement by a joint commission was concluded and signed at Mexico on the 20th day of November, 1843. This treaty was ratified by the United States with certain amendments to which no just exception could have been taken, but it has not yet received the ratification of the Mexican Government. In the meantime our citizens, who suffered great losses-and some of whom have been reduced from affluence to bankruptcy-are without remedy unless their rights be enforced by their Government. Such a continued and unprovoked series of wrongs could never have been tolerated by the United States had they been committed by one of the principal nations of Europe. Mexico was, however, a neighboring sister republic, which, following our example, had achieved her independence, and for whose success and prosperity all our sympathies were early enlisted. The United States were the first to recognize her independence and to receive her into the family of nations, and have ever been desirous of cultivating with her a good understanding. We have therefore borne the repeated wrongs she has committed with great patience, in the hope that a returning sense of justice would ultimately guide her councils and that we might, if possible, honorably avoid any hostile collision with her. Without the previous authority of Congress the Executive possessed no power to adopt or enforce adequate remedies for the injuries we had suffered, or to do more than to be prepared to repel the threatened aggression on the part of Mexico. After our Army and Navy had remained on the frontier and coasts of Mexico for many weeks without any hostile movement on her part, though her menaces were continued, I deemed it important to put an end, if possible, to this state of things. With this view I caused steps to be taken in the month of September last to ascertain distinctly and in an authentic form what the designs of the Mexican Government were-whether it was their intention to declare war, or invade Texas, or whether they were disposed to adjust and settle in an amicable manner the pending differences between the two countries. On the 9th of November an official answer was received that the Mexican Government consented to renew the diplomatic relations which had been suspended in March last, and for that purpose were willing to accredit a minister from the United States. With a sincere desire to preserve peace and restore relations of good understanding between the two Republics, I waived all ceremony as to the manner of renewing diplomatic intercourse between them, and, assuming the initiative, on the 10th of November a distinguished citizen of Louisiana was appointed envoy extraordinary and minister plenipotentiary to Mexico, clothed with full powers to adjust and definitively settle all pending differences between the two countries, including those of boundary between Mexico and the State of Texas. The minister appointed has set out on his mission and is probably by this time near the Mexican capital. He has been instructed to bring the negotiation with which he is charged to a conclusion at the earliest practicable period, which it is expected will be in time to enable me to communicate the result to

Congress during the present session. Until that result is known I forbear to recommend to Congress such ulterior measures of redress for the wrongs and injuries we have so long borne as it would have been proper to make had no such negotiation been instituted.

Congress appropriated at the last session the sum of $275,000 for the payment of the April and July installments of the Mexican indemnities for the year 1844:

Provided it shall be ascertained to the satisfaction of the American Government that said installments have been paid by the Mexican Government to the agent appointed by the United States to receive the same in such manner as to discharge all claim on the Mexican Government, and said agent to be delinquent in remitting the money to the United States.

The unsettled state of our relations with Mexico has involved this subject in much mystery. The first information in an authentic form from the agent of the United States, appointed under the Administration of my predecessor, was received at the State Department on the 9th of November last. This is contained in a letter, dated the 17th of October, addressed by him to one of our citizens then in Mexico with a view of having it communicated to that Department. From this it appears that the agent on the 20th of September, 1844, gave a receipt to the treasury of Mexico for the amount of the April and July installments of the indemnity. In the same communication, however, he asserts that he had not received a single dollar in cash, but that he holds such securities as warranted him at the time in giving the receipt, and entertains no doubt but that he will eventually obtain the money. As these installments appear never to have been actually paid by the Government of Mexico to the agent, and as that Government has not, therefore, been released so as to discharge the claim, I do not feel myself warranted in directing payment to be made to the claimants out of the Treasury without further legislation. Their case is undoubtedly one of much hardship, and it remains for Congress to decide whether any, and what, relief ought to be granted to them. Our minister to Mexico has been instructed to ascertain the facts of the case from the Mexican Government in an authentic and official form and report the result with as little delay as possible.

My attention was early directed to the negotiation which on the 4th of March last I found pending at Washington between the United States and Great Britain on the subject of the Oregon Territory. Three several attempts had been previously made to settle the questions in dispute between the two countries by negotiation upon the principle of compromise, but each had proved unsuccessful. These negotiations took place at London in the years 1818, 1824, and 1826-the two first under the Administration of Mr. Monroe and the last under that of Mr. Adams. The negotiation of 1818, having failed to accomplish its object, resulted in the convention of the 20th of October of that year.

By the third article of that convention it was- Agreed that any country that may be claimed by either party on the northwest coast of America westward of the Stony Mountains shall, together with its harbors, bays, and creeks, and the navigation of all rivers within the same, be free and open for the term of ten years from the date of the signature of the present convention to the vessels, citizens, and subjects of the two powers; it being well understood that this agreement is not to be construed to the prejudice of any claim which either of the two high contracting parties may have to any part of the said country, nor shall it be taken to affect the claims of any other power or state to any part of the said country, the only object of the high contracting parties in that respect being to prevent disputes and differences amongst themselves.

The negotiation of 1824 was productive of no result, and the convention of 1818 was left unchanged. The negotiation of 1826, having also failed to effect an adjustment by compromise, resulted in the convention of August 6, 1827, by which it was agreed to continue in force for an indefinite period the provisions of the third article of the convention of the 20th of October, 1818; and it was further provided that-

It shall be competent, however, to either of the contracting parties, in case either should think fit, at any time after the 20th of October, 1828, on giving due notice of twelve months to the other contracting party, to annul and abrogate this convention; and it shall in such case be accordingly entirely annulled and abrogated after the expiration of the said term of notice.

In these attempts to adjust the controversy the parallel of the forty-ninth degree of north latitude had been offered by the United States to Great Britain, and in those of 1818 and 1826, with a further concession of the free navigation of the Columbia River south of that latitude. The parallel of the forty-ninth degree from the Rocky Mountains to its intersection with the northeasternmost branch of the Columbia, and thence down the channel of that river to the sea, had been offered by Great Britain, with an addition of a small detached territory north of the Columbia. Each of these propositions had been rejected by the parties respectively. In October, 1843, the envoy extraordinary and minister plenipotentiary of the United

States in London was authorized to make a similar offer to those made in 1818 and 1826. Thus stood the question when the negotiation was shortly afterwards transferred to Washington, and on the 23d of August, 1844, was formally opened under the direction of my immediate predecessor. Like all the previous negotiations, it was based upon principles of "compromise," and the avowed purpose of the parties was "to treat of the respective claims of the two countries to the Oregon Territory with the view to establish a permanent boundary between them westward of the Rocky Mountains to the Pacific Ocean."

Accordingly, on the 26th of August, 1844, the British plenipotentiary offered to divide the Oregon Territory by the forty-ninth parallel of north latitude from the Rocky Mountains to the point of its intersection with the northeasternmost branch of the Columbia River, and thence down that river to the sea, leaving the free navigation of the river to be enjoyed in common by both parties, the country south of this line to belong to the United States and that north of it to Great Britain. At the same time he proposed in addition to yield to the United States a detached territory north of the Columbia extending along the Pacific and the Straits of Fuca from Bulfinchs Harbor, inclusive, to Hoods Canal, and to make free to the United States any port or ports south of latitude 49° which they might desire, either on the mainland or on Quadra and Vancouvers Island. With the exception of the free ports, this was the same offer which had been made by the British and rejected by the American Government in the negotiation of 1826. This proposition was properly rejected by the American plenipotentiary on the day it was submitted. This was the only proposition of compromise offered by the British plenipotentiary. The proposition on the part of Great Britain having been rejected, the British plenipotentiary requested that a proposal should be made by the United States for "an equitable adjustment of the question." When I came into office I found this to be the state of the negotiation. Though entertaining the settled conviction that the British pretensions of title could not be maintained to any portion of the Oregon Territory upon any principle of public law recognized by nations, yet in deference to what had been done by my predecessors, and especially in consideration that propositions of compromise had been thrice made by two preceding Administrations to adjust the question on the parallel of 49°, and in two of them yielding to Great Britain the free navigation of the Columbia, and that the pending negotiation had been commenced on the basis of compromise, I deemed it to be my duty not abruptly to break it off. In consideration, too, that under the conventions of 1818 and 1827 the citizens and subjects of the two powers held a joint occupancy of the country, I was induced to make another effort to settle this long-pending controversy in the spirit of moderation which had given birth to the renewed discussion. A proposition was accordingly made, which was rejected by the British plenipotentiary, who, without submitting any other proposition, suffered the negotiation on his part to drop, expressing his trust that the United States would offer what he saw fit to call "some further proposal for the settlement of the Oregon question more consistent with fairness and equity and with the reasonable expectations of the British Government." The proposition thus offered and rejected repeated the offer of the parallel of 49° of north latitude, which had been made by two preceding Administrations, but without proposing to surrender to Great Britain, as they had done, the free navigation of the Columbia River. The right of any foreign power to the free navigation of any of our rivers through the heart of our country was one which I was unwilling to concede. It also embraced a provision to make free to Great Britain any port or ports on the cap of Quadra and Vancouvers Island south of this parallel. Had this been a new question, coming under discussion for the first time, this proposition would not have been made. The extraordinary and wholly inadmissible demands of the British Government and the rejection of the proposition made in deference alone to what had been done by my predecessors and the implied obligation which their acts seemed to impose afford satisfactory evidence that no compromise which the United States ought to accept can be effected. With this conviction the proposition of compromise which had been made and rejected was by my direction subsequently withdrawn and our title to the whole Oregon Territory asserted, and, as is believed, maintained by irrefragable facts and arguments.

The civilized world will see in these proceedings a spirit of liberal concession on the part of the United States, and this Government will be relieved from all responsibility which may follow the failure to settle the controversy.

All attempts at compromise having failed, it becomes the duty of Congress to consider what measures it may be proper to adopt for the security and protection of our citizens now inhabiting or who may hereafter inhabit Oregon, and for the maintenance of our just title to that Territory. In adopting measures for this purpose care should be taken that nothing be done to violate the stipulations of the convention of 1827, which is still in force. The faith of treaties, in their letter and spirit, has ever been, and, I trust, will ever be, scrupulously observed by the United States. Under that convention a year's notice is required to be given by either party to the other before the joint occupancy shall terminate and before either can rightfully assert or exercise exclusive jurisdiction over any portion of the territory. This notice it would, in my judgment, be proper to give, and I recommend that provision be made by law for giving it accordingly, and terminating in this manner the convention of the 6th of August, 1827.

It will become proper for Congress to determine what legislation they can in the meantime adopt without violating this convention. Beyond all question the protection of our laws and our jurisdiction, civil and criminal, ought to be immediately extended over our citizens in Oregon. They have had just cause to complain of our long neglect in this particular, and have in consequence been compelled for their own security and protection to establish a provisional government for themselves. Strong in their allegiance and ardent in their attachment to the United States, they have been thus cast upon their own resources. They are anxious that our laws should be extended over them, and I recommend that this be done by Congress with as little delay as possible in the full extent to which the British Parliament have proceeded in regard to British subjects in that Territory by their act of July 2, 1821, "for regulating the fur trade and establishing a criminal and civil jurisdiction within certain parts of North America." By this act Great Britain extended her laws and jurisdiction, civil and criminal, over her subjects engaged in the fur trade in that Territory. By it the courts of the Province of Upper Canada were empowered to take cognizance of causes civil and criminal. Justices of the peace and other judicial officers were authorized to be appointed in Oregon with power to execute all process issuing from the courts of that Province, and to "sit and hold courts of record for the trial of criminal offenses and misdemeanors" not made the subject of capital punishment, and also of civil eases where the cause of action shall not "exceed in value the amount or sum of lbs. 200."

Subsequent to the date of this act of Parliament a grant was made from the "British Crown" to the Hudsons Bay Company of the exclusive trade with the Indian tribes in the Oregon Territory, subject to a reservation that it shall not operate to the exclusion "of the subjects of any foreign states who, under or by force of any convention for the time being between us and such foreign states, respectively, may be entitled to and shall be engaged in the said trade." It is much to be regretted that while under this act British subjects have enjoyed the protection of British laws and British judicial tribunals throughout the whole of Oregon, American citizens in the same Territory have enjoyed no such protection from their Government. At the same time, the result illustrates the character of our people and their institutions. In spite of this neglect they have multiplied, and their number is rapidly increasing in that Territory. They have made no appeal to arms, but have peacefully fortified themselves in their new homes by the adoption of republican institutions for themselves, furnishing another example of the truth that self-government is inherent in the American breast and must prevail. It is due to them that they should be embraced and protected by our laws. It is deemed important that our laws regulating trade and intercourse with the Indian tribes east of the Rocky Mountains should be extended to such tribes as dwell beyond them. The increasing emigration to Oregon and the care and protection which is due from the Government to its citizens in that distant region make it our duty, as it is our interest, to cultivate amicable relations with the Indian tribes of that Territory. For this purpose I recommend that provision be made for establishing an Indian agency and such subagencies as may be deemed necessary beyond the Rocky Mountains.

For the protection of emigrants whilst on their way to Oregon against the attacks of the Indian tribes occupying the country through which they pass, I recommend that a suitable number of stockades and blockhouse forts be erected along the usual route between our frontier settlements on the Missouri and the Rocky Mountains, and that an adequate force of mounted riflemen be raised to guard and protect them on their journey. The immediate adoption of these recommendations by Congress will not violate the provisions of the existing treaty. It will be doing nothing more for American citizens than British laws have long since done for British subjects in the same territory.

It requires several months to perform the voyage by sea from the Atlantic States to Oregon, and although we have a large number of whale ships in the Pacific, but few of them afford an opportunity of interchanging intelligence without great delay between our settlements in that distant region and the United States. An overland mail is believed to be entirely practicable, and the importance of establishing such a mail at least once a month is submitted to the favorable consideration of Congress.

It is submitted to the wisdom of Congress to determine whether at their present session, and until after the expiration of the year's notice, any other measures may be adopted consistently with the convention of 1827 for the security of our rights and the government and protection of our citizens in Oregon. That it will ultimately be wise and proper to make liberal grants of land to the patriotic pioneers who amidst privations and dangers lead the way through savage tribes inhabiting the vast wilderness intervening between our frontier settlements and Oregon, and who cultivate and are ever ready to defend the soil, I am fully satisfied. To doubt whether they will obtain such grants as soon as the convention between the United States and Great Britain shall have ceased to exist would be to doubt the justice of Congress; but, pending the year's notice, it is worthy of consideration whether a stipulation to this effect may be made consistently with the spirit of that convention.

The recommendations which I have made as to the best manner of securing our rights in Oregon are submitted to Congress with great deference. Should they in their wisdom devise any other mode better calculated to accomplish the same object, it shall meet with my hearty concurrence.

At the end of the year's notice, should Congress think it proper to make provision for giving that notice, we shall have reached a period when the national rights in Oregon must either be abandoned or firmly maintained. That they can not be abandoned without a sacrifice of both national honor and interest is too clear to admit of doubt.

Oregon is a part of the North American continent, to which, it is confidently affirmed, the title of the United States is the best now in existence. For the grounds on which that title rests I refer you to the correspondence of the late and present Secretary of State with the British plenipotentiary during the negotiation. The British proposition of compromise, which would make the Columbia the line south of 49°, with a trifling addition of detached territory to the United States north of that river, and would leave on the British side two-thirds of the whole Oregon Territory, including the free navigation of the Columbia and all the valuable harbors on the Pacific, can never for a moment be entertained by the United States without an abandonment of their just and dear territorial rights, their own self-respect, and the national honor. For the information of Congress, I communicate herewith the correspondence which took place between the two Governments during the late negotiation.

The rapid extension of our settlements over our territories heretofore unoccupied, the addition of new States to our Confederacy, the expansion of free principles, and our rising greatness as a nation are attracting the attention of the powers of Europe, and lately the doctrine has been broached in some of them of a "balance of power" on this continent to check our advancement. The United States, sincerely desirous of preserving relations of good understanding with all nations, can not in silence permit any European interference on the North American continent, and should any such interference be attempted will be ready to resist it at any and all hazards.

It is well known to the American people and to all nations that this Government has never interfered with the relations subsisting between other governments. We have never made ourselves parties to their wars or their alliances; we have not sought their territories by conquest; we have not mingled with parties in their domestic struggles; and believing our own form of government to be the best, we have never attempted to propagate it by intrigues, by diplomacy, or by force. We may claim on this continent a like exemption from European interference. The nations of America are equally sovereign and independent with those of Europe. They possess the same rights, independent of all foreign interposition, to make war, to conclude peace, and to regulate their internal affairs. The people of the United States can not, therefore, view with indifference attempts of European powers to interfere with the independent action of the nations on this continent. The American system of government is entirely different from that of Europe. Jealousy among the different sovereigns of Europe, lest any one of them might become too powerful for the rest, has caused them anxiously to desire the establishment of what they term the "balance of power." It can not be permitted to have any application on the North American continent, and especially to the United States. We must ever maintain the principle that the people of this continent alone have the right to decide their own destiny. Should any portion of them, constituting an independent state, propose to unite themselves with our Confederacy, this will be a question for them and us to determine without any foreign interposition. We can never consent that European powers shall interfere to prevent such a union because it might disturb the "balance of power" which they may desire to maintain upon this continent. Near a quarter of a century ago the principle was distinctly announced to the world, in the annual message of one of my predecessors, that-

The American continents, by the free and independent condition which they have assumed and maintain, are henceforth not to be considered as subjects for colonization by any European powers.

This principle will apply with greatly increased force should any European power attempt to establish any new colony in North America. In the existing circumstances of the world the present is deemed a proper occasion to reiterate and reaffirm the principle avowed by Mr. Monroe and to state my cordial concurrence in its wisdom and sound policy. The reassertion of this principle, especially in reference to North America, is at this day but the promulgation of a policy which no European power should cherish the disposition to resist. Existing rights of every European nation should be respected, but it is due alike to our safety and our interests that the efficient protection of our laws should be extended over our whole territorial limits, and that it should be distinctly announced to the world as our settled policy that no future European colony or dominion shall with our consent be planted or established on any part of the North American continent.

A question has recently arisen under the tenth article of the subsisting treaty between the United States and Prussia. By this article the consuls of the two countries have the right to sit as judges and arbitrators "in such differences as may arise between the captains and crews of the vessels belonging to the nation whose interests are committed to their charge without the interference of the local authorities, unless the conduct of the crews or of the captain should disturb the order or tranquillity of the country, or the said consuls should require their assistance to cause their decisions to be carried into effect or supported."

The Prussian consul at New Bedford in June, 1844, applied to Mr. Justice Story to carry into effect a decision made by him between the captain and crew of the Prussian ship Borussia, but the request was refused on the ground that without previous legislation by Congress the judiciary did not possess the power to give effect to this article of the treaty. The Prussian Government, through their minister here, have complained of this violation of the treaty, and have asked the Government of the United States to adopt the necessary measures to prevent similar violations hereafter. Good faith to Prussia, as well as to other nations with whom we have similar treaty stipulations, requires that these should be faithfully observed. I have deemed it proper, therefore, to lay the subject before Congress and to recommend such legislation as may be necessary to give effect to these treaty obligations.

By virtue of an arrangement made between the Spanish Government and that of the United States in December, 1831, American vessels, since the 29th of April, 1832, have been admitted to entry in the ports of Spain, including those of the Balearic and Canary islands, on payment of the same tonnage duty of 5 cents per ton, as though they had been Spanish vessels; and this whether our vessels arrive in Spain directly from the United States or indirectly from any other country. When Congress, by the act of 13th July, 1832, gave effect to this arrangement between the two Governments, they confined the reduction of tonnage duty merely to Spanish vessels "coming from a port in Spain," leaving the former discriminating duty to remain against such vessels coming from a port in any other country. It is manifestly unjust that whilst American vessels arriving in the ports of Spain from other countries pay no more duty than Spanish vessels, Spanish vessels arriving in the ports of the United States from other countries should be subjected to heavy discriminating tonnage duties. This is neither equality nor reciprocity, and is in violation of the arrangement concluded in December, 1831, between the two countries. The Spanish Government have made repeated and earnest remonstrances against this inequality, and the favorable attention of Congress has been several times invoked to the subject by my predecessors. I recommend, as an act of justice to Spain, that this inequality be removed by Congress and that the discriminating duties which have been levied under the act of the 13th of July, 1832, on Spanish vessels coming to the United States from any other foreign country be refunded. This recommendation does not embrace Spanish vessels arriving in the United States from Cuba and Porto Rico, which will still remain subject to the provisions of the act of June 30, 1834, concerning tonnage duty on such vessels. By the act of the 14th of July, 1832, coffee was exempted from duty altogether. This exemption was universal, without reference to the country where it was produced or the national character of the vessel in which it was imported. By the tariff act of the 30th of August, 1842, this exemption from duty was restricted to coffee imported in American vessels from the place of its production, whilst coffee imported under all other circumstances was subjected to a duty of 20 per cent ad valorem. Under this act and our existing treaty with the King of the Netherlands Java coffee imported from the European ports of that Kingdom into the United States, whether in Dutch or American vessels, now pays this rate of duty. The Government of the Netherlands complains that such a discriminating duty should have been imposed on coffee the production of one of its colonies, and which is chiefly brought from Java to the ports of that Kingdom and exported from thence to foreign countries. Our trade with the Netherlands is highly beneficial to both countries and our relations with them have ever been of the most friendly character. Under all the circumstances of the case, I recommend that this discrimination should be abolished and that the coffee of Java imported from the Netherlands be placed upon the same footing with that imported directly from Brazil and other countries where it is produced.

Under the eighth section of the tariff act of the 30th of August, 1842, a duty of 15 cents per gallon was imposed on port wine in casks, while on the red wines of several other countries, when imported in casks, a duty of only 6 cents per gallon was imposed. This discrimination, so far as regarded the port wine of Portugal, was deemed a violation of our treaty with that power, which provides that-

No higher or other duties shall be imposed on the importation into the United States of America of any article the growth, produce, or manufacture of the Kingdom and possessions of Portugal than such as are or shall be payable on the like article being the growth, produce, or manufacture of any other foreign country.

Accordingly, to give effect to the treaty as well as to the intention of

Congress, expressed in a proviso to the tariff act itself, that nothing therein contained should be so construed as to interfere with subsisting treaties with foreign nations, a Treasury circular was issued on the 16th of July, 1844, which, among other things, declared the duty on the port wine of Portugal, in casks, under the existing laws and treaty to be 6 cents per gallon, and directed that the excess of duties which had been collected on such wine should be refunded. By virtue of another clause in the same section of the act it is provided that all imitations of port or any other wines "shall be subject to the duty provided for the genuine article." Imitations of port wine, the production of France, are imported to some extent into the United States, and the Government of that country now claims that under a correct construction of the act these imitations ought not to pay a higher duty than that imposed upon the original port wine of Portugal. It appears to me to be unequal and unjust that French imitations of port wine should be subjected to a duty of 15 cents, while the more valuable article from Portugal should pay a duty of 6 cents only per gallon. I therefore recommend to Congress such legislation as may be necessary to correct the inequality.

The late President, in his annual message of December last, recommended an appropriation to satisfy the claims of the Texan Government against the United States, which had been previously adjusted so far as the powers of the Executive extend. These claims arose out of the act of disarming a body of Texan troops under the command of Major Snively by an officer in the service of the United States, acting under the orders of our Government, and the forcible entry into the custom-house at Bryarlys Landing, on Red River, by certain citizens of the United States and taking away therefrom the goods seized by the collector of the customs as forfeited under the laws of Texas. This was a liquidated debt ascertained to be due to Texas when an independent state. Her acceptance of the terms of annexation proposed by the United States does not discharge or invalidate the claim. I recommend that provision be made for its payment.

The commissioner appointed to China during the special session of the Senate in March last shortly afterwards set out on his mission in the United States ship Columbus. On arriving at Rio de Janeiro on his passage the state of his health had become so critical that by the advice of his medical attendants he returned to the United States early in the month of October last. Commodore Biddle, commanding the East India Squadron, proceeded on his voyage in the Columbus, and was charged by the commissioner with the duty of exchanging with the proper authorities the ratifications of the treaty lately concluded with the Emperor of China. Since the return of the commissioner to the United States his health has been much improved, and he entertains the confident belief that he will soon be able to proceed on his mission.

Unfortunately, differences continue to exist among some of the nations of South America which, following our example, have established their independence, while in others internal dissensions prevail. It is natural that our sympathies should be warmly enlisted for their welfare; that we should desire that all controversies between them should be amicably adjusted and their Governments administered in a manner to protect the rights and promote the prosperity of their people. It is contrary, however, to our settled policy to interfere in their controversies, whether external or internal.

I have thus adverted to all the subjects connected with our foreign relations to which I deem it necessary to call your attention. Our policy is not only peace with all, but good will toward all the powers of the earth. While we are just to all, we require that all shall be just to us. Excepting the differences with Mexico and Great Britain, our relations with all civilized nations are of the most satisfactory character. It is hoped that in this enlightened age these differences may be amicably adjusted.

The Secretary of the Treasury in his annual report to Congress will communicate a full statement of the condition of our finances. The imports for the fiscal year ending on the 30th of June last were of the value of $117,254,564, of which the amount exported was $15,346,830, leaving a balance of $101,907,734 for domestic consumption. The exports for the same year were of the value of $114,646,606, of which the amount of domestic articles was $99,299,776. The receipts into the Treasury during the same year were $29,769,133.56, of which there were derived from customs $27,528,122.70, from sales of public lands $2,077,022.30, and from incidental and miscellaneous sources $163,998.56. The expenditures for the same period were $29,968,206.98, of which $8,588,157.62 were applied to the payment of the public debt. The balance in the Treasury on the 1st of July last was $7,658,306.22. The amount of the public debt remaining unpaid on the 1st of October last was $17,075,445.52. Further payments of the public debt would have been made, in anticipation of the period of its reimbursement under the authority conferred upon the Secretary of the Treasury by the acts of July 21, 1841, and of April 15, 1842, and March 3, 1843, had not the unsettled state of our relations with Mexico menaced hostile collision with that power. In view of such a contingency it was deemed prudent to retain in the Treasury an amount unusually large for ordinary purposes.

A few years ago our whole national debt growing out of the Revolution and the War of 1812 with Great Britain was extinguished, and we presented to the world the rare and noble spectacle of a great and growing people who had fully discharged every obligation. Since that time the existing debt has been contracted, and, small as it is in comparison with the similar burdens of most other nations, it should be extinguished at the earliest practicable period. Should the state of the country permit, and especially if our foreign relations interpose no obstacle, it is contemplated to apply all the moneys in the Treasury as they accrue, beyond what is required for the appropriations by Congress, to its liquidation. I cherish the hope of soon being able to congratulate the country on its recovering once more the lofty position which it so recently occupied. Our country, which exhibits to the world the benefits of self-government, in developing all the sources of national prosperity owes to mankind the permanent example of a nation free from the blighting influence of a public debt.

The attention of Congress is invited to the importance of making suitable modifications and reductions of the rates of duty imposed by our present tariff laws. The object of imposing duties on imports should be to raise revenue to pay the necessary expenses of Government. Congress may undoubtedly, in the exercise of a sound discretion, discriminate in arranging the rates of duty on different articles, but the discriminations should be within the revenue standard and be made with the view to raise money for the support of Government.

It becomes important to understand distinctly what is meant by a revenue standard the maximum of which should not be exceeded in the rates of duty imposed. It is conceded, and experience proves, that duties may be laid so high as to diminish or prohibit altogether the importation of any given article, and thereby lessen or destroy the revenue which at lower rates would be derived from its importation. Such duties exceed the revenue rates and are not imposed to raise money for the support of Government. If Congress levy a duty for revenue of 1 per cent on a given article, it will produce a given amount of money to the Treasury and will incidentally and necessarily afford protection or advantage to the amount of 1 per cent to the home manufacturer of a similar or like article over the importer. If the duty be raised to 10 per cent, it will produce a greater amount of money and afford greater protection. If it be still raised to 20, 25, or 30 per cent, and if as it is raised the revenue derived from it is found to be increased, the protection or advantage will also be increased; but if it be raised to 31 per cent, and it is found that the revenue produced at that rate is less than at 30 per cent, it ceases to be a revenue duty. The precise point in the ascending scale of duties at which it is ascertained from experience that the revenue is greatest is the maximum rate of duty which can be laid for the bona fide purpose of collecting money for the support of Government. To raise the duties higher than that point, and thereby diminish the amount collected, is to levy them for protection merely, and not for revenue. As long, then, as Congress may gradually increase the rate of duty on a given article, and the revenue is increased by such increase of duty, they are within the revenue standard. When they go beyond that point, and as they increase the duties, the revenue is diminished or destroyed; the act ceases to have for its object the raising of money to support Government, but is for protection merely. It does not follow that Congress should levy the highest duty on all articles of import which they will bear within the revenue standard, for such rates would probably produce a much larger amount than the economical administration of the Government would require. Nor does it follow that the duties on all articles should be at the same or a horizontal rate. Some articles will bear a much higher revenue duty than others. Below the maximum of the revenue standard Congress may and ought to discriminate in the rates imposed, taking care so to adjust them on different articles as to produce in the aggregate the amount which, when added to the proceeds of the sales of public lands, may be needed to pay the economical expenses of the Government.

In levying a tariff of duties Congress exercise the taxing power, and for purposes of revenue may select the objects of taxation. They may exempt certain articles altogether and permit their importation free of duty. On others they may impose low duties. In these classes should be embraced such articles of necessity as are in general use, and especially such as are consumed by the laborer and poor as well as by the wealthy citizen. Care should be taken that all the great interests of the country, including manufactures, agriculture, commerce, navigation, and the mechanic arts, should, as far as may be practicable, derive equal advantages from the incidental protection which a just system of revenue duties may afford. Taxation, direct or indirect, is a burden, and it should be so imposed as to operate as equally as may be on all classes in the proportion of their ability to bear it. To make the taxing power an actual benefit to one class necessarily increases the burden of the others beyond their proportion, and would be manifestly unjust. The terms "protection to domestic industry" are of popular import, but they should apply under a just system to all the various branches of industry in our country. The farmer or planter who toils yearly in his fields is engaged in "domestic industry," and is as much entitled to have his labor "protected" as the manufacturer, the man of commerce, the navigator, or the mechanic, who are engaged also in "domestic industry" in their different pursuits. The joint labors of all these classes constitute the aggregate of the "domestic industry" of the nation, and they are equally entitled to the nation's "protection." No one of them can justly claim to be the exclusive recipient of "protection," which can only be afforded by increasing burdens on the "domestic industry" of the others.

If these views be correct, it remains to inquire how far the tariff act of 1842 is consistent with them. That many of the provisions of that act are in violation of the cardinal principles here laid down all must concede. The rates of duty imposed by it on some articles are prohibitory and on others so high as greatly to diminish importations and to produce a less amount of revenue than would be derived from lower rates. They operate as "protection merely" to one branch of "domestic industry" by taxing other branches.

By the introduction of minimums, or assumed and false values, and by the imposition of specific duties the injustice and inequality of the act of 1842 in its practical operations on different classes and pursuits are seen and felt. Many of the oppressive duties imposed by it under the operation of these principles range from 1 per cent to more than 200 per cent. They are prohibitory on some articles and partially so on others, and bear most heavily on articles of common necessity and but lightly on articles of luxury. It is so framed that much the greatest burden which it imposes is thrown on labor and the poorer classes, who are least able to bear it, while it protects capital and exempts the rich from paying their just proportion of the taxation required for the support of Government. While it protects the capital of the wealthy manufacturer and increases his profits, it does not benefit the operatives or laborers in his employment, whose wages have not been increased by it. Articles of prime necessity or of coarse quality and low price, used by the masses of the people, are in many instances subjected by it to heavy taxes, while articles of finer quality and higher price, or of luxury, which can be used only by the opulent, are lightly taxed. It imposes heavy and unjust burdens on the farmer, the planter, the commercial man, and those of all other pursuits except the capitalist who has made his investments in manufactures. All the great interests of the country are not as nearly as may be practicable equally protected by it.

The Government in theory knows no distinction of persons or classes, and should not bestow upon some favors and privileges which all others may not enjoy. It was the purpose of its illustrious founders to base the institutions which they reared upon the great and unchanging principles of justice and equity, conscious that if administered in the spirit in which they were conceived they would be felt only by the benefits which they diffused, and would secure for themselves a defense in the hearts of the people more powerful than standing armies and all the means and appliances invented to sustain governments founded in injustice and oppression.

The well-known fact that the tariff act of 1842 was passed by a majority of one vote in the Senate and two in the House of Representatives, and that some of those who felt themselves constrained, under the peculiar circumstances existing at the time, to vote in its favor, proclaimed its defects and expressed their determination to aid in its modification on the first opportunity, affords strong and conclusive evidence that it was not intended to be permanent, and of the expediency and necessity of its thorough revision.

In recommending to Congress a reduction of the present rates of duty and a revision and modification of the act of 1842, I am far from entertaining opinions unfriendly to the manufacturers. On the contrary, I desire to see them prosperous as far as they can be so without imposing unequal burdens on other interests. The advantage under any system of indirect taxation, even within the revenue standard, must be in favor of the manufacturing interest, and of this no other interest will complain.

I recommend to Congress the abolition of the minimum principle, or assumed, arbitrary, and false values, and of specific duties, and the substitution in their place of ad valorem duties as the fairest and most equitable indirect tax which can be imposed. By the ad valorem principle all articles are taxed according to their cost or value, and those which are of inferior quality or of small cost bear only the just proportion of the tax with those which are of superior quality or greater cost. The articles consumed by all are taxed at the same rate. A system of ad valorem revenue duties, with proper discriminations and proper guards against frauds in collecting them, it is not doubted will afford ample incidental advantages to the manufacturers and enable them to derive as great profits as can be derived from any other regular business. It is believed that such a system strictly within the revenue standard will place the manufacturing interests on a stable footing and inure to their permanent advantage, while it will as nearly as may be practicable extend to all the great interests of the country the incidental protection which can be afforded by our revenue laws. Such a system, when once firmly established, would be permanent, and not be subject to the constant complaints, agitations, and changes which must ever occur when duties are not laid for revenue, but for the "protection merely" of a favored interest.

In the deliberations of Congress on this subject it is hoped that a spirit of mutual concession and compromise between conflicting interests may prevail, and that the result of their labors may be crowned with the happiest consequences.

By the Constitution of the United States it is provided that "no money shall be drawn from the Treasury but in consequence of appropriations made by law." A public treasury was undoubtedly contemplated and intended to be created, in which the public money should be kept from the period of collection until needed for public uses. In the collection and disbursement of the public money no agencies have ever been employed by law except such as were appointed by the Government, directly responsible to it and under its control. The safe-keeping of the public money should be confided to a public treasury created by law and under like responsibility and control. It is not to be imagined that the framers of the Constitution could have intended that a treasury should be created as a place of deposit and safe-keeping of the public money which was irresponsible to the Government. The first Congress under the Constitution, by the act of the 2d of September, 1789, "to establish the Treasury Department," provided for the appointment of a Treasurer, and made it his duty "to receive and keep the moneys of the United States" and "at all times to submit to the Secretary of the Treasury and the Comptroller, or either of them, the inspection of the moneys in his hands."

That banks, national or State, could not have been intended to be used as a substitute for the Treasury spoken of in the Constitution as keepers of the public money is manifest from the fact that at that time there was no national bank, and but three or four State banks, of limited Capital, existed in the country. Their employment as depositories was at first resorted to to a limited extent, but with no avowed intention of continuing them permanently in place of the Treasury of the Constitution. When they were afterwards from time to time employed, it was from motives of supposed convenience. Our experience has shown that when banking corporations have been the keepers of the public money, and been thereby made in effect the Treasury, the Government can have no guaranty that it can command the use of its own money for public purposes. The late Bank of the United States proved to be faithless. The State banks which were afterwards employed were faithless. But a few years ago, with millions of public money in their keeping, the Government was brought almost to bankruptcy and the public credit seriously impaired because of their inability or indisposition to pay on demand to the public creditors in the only currency recognized by the Constitution. Their failure occurred in a period of peace, and great inconvenience and loss were suffered by the public from it. Had the country been involved in a foreign war, that inconvenience and loss would have been much greater, and might have resulted in extreme public calamity. The public money should not be mingled with the private funds of banks or individuals or be used for private purposes. When it is placed in banks for safe-keeping, it is in effect loaned to them without interest, and is loaned by them upon interest to the borrowers from them. The public money is converted into banking capital, and is used and loaned out for the private profit of bank stockholders, and when called for, as was the case in 1837, it may be in the pockets of the borrowers from the banks instead of being in the public Treasury contemplated by the Constitution. The framers of the Constitution could never have intended that the money paid into the Treasury should be thus converted to private use and placed beyond the control of the Government.

Banks which hold the public money are often tempted by a desire of gain to extend their loans, increase their circulation, and thus stimulate, if not produce, a spirit of speculation and extravagance which sooner or later must result in ruin to thousands. If the public money be not permitted to be thus used, but be kept in the Treasure and paid out to the public creditors in gold and silver, the temptation afforded by its deposit with banks to an undue expansion of their business would be checked, while the amount of the constitutional currency left in circulation would be enlarged by its employment in the public collections and disbursements, and the banks themselves would in consequence be found in a safer and sounder condition. At present State banks are employed as depositories, but without adequate regulation of law whereby the public money can be secured against the casualties and excesses, revulsions, suspensions, and defalcations to which from overissues, overtrading, an inordinate desire for gain, or other causes they are constantly exposed. The Secretary of the Treasury has in all cases when it was practicable taken collateral security for the amount which they hold, by the pledge of stocks of the United States or such of the States as were in good credit. Some of the deposit banks have given this description of security and others have declined to do so.

Entertaining the opinion that "the separation of the moneys of the Government from banking institutions is indispensable for the safety of the funds of the Government and the rights of the people," I recommend to Congress that provision be made by law for such separation, and that a constitutional treasury be created for the safe-keeping of the public money. The constitutional treasury recommended is designed as a secure depository for the public money, without any power to make loans or discounts or to issue any paper whatever as a currency or circulation. I can not doubt that such a treasury as was contemplated by the Constitution should be independent of all banking corporations. The money of the people should be kept in the Treasury of the people created by law, and be in the custody of agents of the people chosen by themselves according to the forms of the

Constitution-agents who are directly responsible to the Government, who are under adequate bonds and oaths, and who are subject to severe punishments for any embezzlement, private use, or misapplication of the public funds, and for any failure in other respects to perform their duties. To say that the people or their Government are incompetent or not to be trusted with the custody of their own money in their own Treasury, provided by themselves, but must rely on the presidents, cashiers, and stockholders of banking corporations, not appointed by them nor responsible to them, would be to concede that they are incompetent for self-government.

In recommending the establishment of a constitutional treasury in which the public money shall be kept, I desire that adequate provision be made by law for its safety and that all Executive discretion or control over it shall be removed, except such as may be necessary in directing its disbursement in pursuance of appropriations made by law.

Under our present land system, limiting the minimum price at which the public lands can be entered to $1.25 per acre, large quantities of lands of inferior quality remain unsold because they will not command that price. From the records of the General Land Office it appears that of the public lands remaining unsold in the several States and Territories in which they are situated, 39,105,577 acres have been in the market subject to entry more than twenty years, 49,638,644 acres for more than fifteen years, 73,074,600 acres for more than ten years, and 106,176,961 acres for more than five years. Much the largest portion of these lands will continue to be unsalable at the minimum price at which they are permitted to be sold so long as large territories of lands from which the more valuable portions have not been selected are annually brought into market by the Government. With the view to the sale and settlement of these inferior lands, I recommend that the price be graduated and reduced below the present minimum rate, confining the sales at the reduced prices to settlers and cultivators, in limited quantities. If graduated and reduced in price for a limited term to $1 per acre, and after the expiration of that period for a second and third term to lower rates, a large portion of these lands would be purchased, and many worthy citizens who are unable to pay higher rates could purchase homes for themselves and their families. By adopting the policy of graduation and reduction of price these inferior lands will be sold for their real value, while the States in which they lie will be freed from the inconvenience, if not injustice, to which they are subjected in consequence of the United States continuing to own large quantities of the public lands within their borders not liable to taxation for the support of their local governments.

I recommend the continuance of the policy of granting preemptions in its most liberal extent to all those who have settled or may hereafter settle on the public lands, whether surveyed or unsurveyed, to which the Indian title may have been extinguished at the time of settlement. It has been found by experience that in consequence of combinations of purchasers and other causes a very small quantity of the public lands, when sold at public auction, commands a higher price than the minimum rates established by law. The settlers on the public lands are, however, but rarely able to secure their homes and improvements at the public sales at that rate, because these combinations, by means of the capital they command and their superior ability to purchase, render it impossible for the settler to compete with them in the market. By putting down all competition these combinations of capitalists and speculators are usually enabled to purchase the lands, including the improvements of the settlers, at the minimum price of the Government, and either turn them out of their homes or extort from them, according to their ability to pay, double or quadruple the amount paid for them to the Government. It is to the enterprise and perseverance of the hardy pioneers of the West, who penetrate the wilderness with their families, suffer the dangers, the privations, and hardships attending the settlement of a new country, and prepare the way for the body of emigrants who in the course of a few years usually follow them, that we are in a great degree indebted for the rapid extension and aggrandizement of our country.

Experience has proved that no portion of our population are more patriotic than the hardy and brave men of the frontier, or more ready to obey the call of their country and to defend her rights and her honor whenever and by whatever enemy assailed. They should be protected from the grasping speculator and secured, at the minimum price of the public lands, in the humble homes which they have improved by their labor. With this end in view, all vexatious or unnecessary restrictions imposed upon them by the existing preemption laws should be repealed or modified. It is the true policy of the Government to afford facilities to its citizens to become the owners of small portions of our vast public domain at low and moderate rates.

The present system of managing the mineral lands of the United States is believed to be radically defective. More than 1,000,000 acres of the public lands, supposed to contain lead and other minerals, have been reserved from sale, and numerous leases upon them have been granted to individuals upon a stipulated rent. The system of granting leases has proved to be not only unprofitable to the Government, but unsatisfactory to the citizens who have gone upon the lands, and must, if continued, lay the foundation of much future difficulty between the Government and the lessees. According to the official records, the amount of rents received by the Government for the years 1841, 1842, 1843, and 1844 was $6,354.74, while the expenses of the system during the same period, including salaries of superintendents, agents, clerks, and incidental expenses, were $26,111.11, the income being less than one-fourth of the expenses. To this pecuniary loss may be added the injury sustained by the public in consequence of the destruction of timber and the careless and wasteful manner of working the mines. The system has given rise to much litigation between the United States and individual citizens, producing irritation and excitement in the mineral region, and involving the Government in heavy additional expenditures. It is believed that similar losses and embarrassments will continue to occur while the present System of leasing these lands remains unchanged. These lands are now under the superintendence and care of the War Department, with the ordinary duties of which they have no proper or natural connection. I recommend the repeal of the present system, and that these lands be placed under the superintendence and management of the General Land Office, as other public lands, and be brought into market and sold upon such terms as Congress in their wisdom may prescribe, reserving to the Government an equitable percentage of the gross amount of mineral product, and that the preemption principle be extended to resident miners and settlers upon them at the minimum price which may be established by Congress.

I refer you to the accompanying report of the Secretary of War for information respecting the present situation of the Army and its operations during the past year, the state of our defenses, the condition of the public works, and our relations with the various Indian tribes within our limits or upon our borders. I invite your attention to the suggestions contained in that report in relation to these prominent objects of national interest. When orders were given during the past summer for concentrating a military force on the western frontier of Texas, our troops were widely dispersed and in small detachments, occupying posts remote from each other. The prompt and expeditious manner in which an army embracing more than half our peace establishment was drawn together on an emergency so sudden reflects great credit on the officers who were intrusted with the execution of these orders, as well as upon the discipline of the Army itself. To be in strength to protect and defend the people and territory of Texas in the event Mexico should commence hostilities or invade her territories with a large army, which she threatened, I authorized the general assigned to the command of the army of occupation to make requisitions for additional forces from several of the States nearest the Texan territory, and which could most expeditiously furnish them, if in his opinion a larger force than that under his command and the auxiliary aid which under like circumstances he was authorized to receive from Texas should be required. The contingency upon which the exercise of this authority depended has not occurred. The circumstances under which two companies of State artillery from the city of New Orleans were sent into Texas and mustered into the service of the United States are fully stated in the report of the Secretary of War. I recommend to Congress that provision be made for the payment of these troops, as well as a small number of Texan volunteers whom the commanding general thought it necessary to receive or muster into our service.

During the last summer the First Regiment of Dragoons made extensive excursions through the Indian country on our borders, a part of them advancing nearly to the possessions of the Hudsons Bay Company in the north, and a part as far as the South Pass of the Rocky Mountains and the head waters of the tributary streams of the Colorado of the West. The exhibition of this military force among the Indian tribes in those distant regions and the councils held with them by the commanders of the expeditions, it is believed, will have a salutary influence in restraining them from hostilities among themselves and maintaining friendly relations between them and the United States. An interesting account of one of these excursions accompanies the report of the Secretary of War. Under the directions of the War Department Brevet Captain Fremont, of the Corps of Topographical Engineers, has been employed since 1842 in exploring the country west of the Mississippi and beyond the Rocky Mountains. Two expeditions have already been brought to a close, and the reports of that scientific and enterprising officer have furnished much interesting and valuable information. He is now engaged in a third expedition, but it is not expected that this arduous service will be completed in season to enable me to communicate the result to Congress at the present session.

Our relations with the Indian tribes are of a favorable character. The policy of removing them to a country designed for their permanent residence west of the Mississippi, and without the limits of the organized States and Territories, is better appreciated by them than it was a few years ago, while education is now attended to and the habits of civilized life are gaining ground among them.

Serious difficulties of long standing continue to distract the several parties into which the Cherokees are unhappily divided. The efforts of the Government to adjust the difficulties between them have heretofore proved unsuccessful, and there remains no probability that this desirable object can be accomplished without the aid of further legislation by Congress. I will at an early period of your session present the subject for your consideration, accompanied with an exposition of the complaints and claims of the several parties into which the nation is divided, with a view to the adoption of such measures by Congress as may enable the Executive to do justice to them, respectively, and to put an end, if possible, to the dissensions which have long prevailed and still prevail among them.

I refer you to the report of the Secretary of the Navy for the present condition of that branch of the national defense and for grave suggestions having for their object the increase of its efficiency and a greater economy in its management. During the past year the officers and men have performed their duty in a satisfactory manner. The orders which have been given have been executed with promptness and fidelity. A larger force than has often formed one squadron under our flag was readily concentrated in the Gulf of Mexico, and apparently without unusual effort. It is especially to be observed that notwithstanding the union of so considerable a force, no act was committed that even the jealousy of an irritated power could construe as an act of aggression, and that the commander of the squadron and his officers, in strict conformity with their instructions, holding themselves ever ready for the most active duty, have achieved the still purer glory of contributing to the preservation of peace. It is believed that at all our foreign stations the honor of our flag has been maintained and that generally our ships of war have been distinguished for their good discipline and order. I am happy to add that the display of maritime force which was required by the events of the summer has been made wholly within the usual appropriations for the service of the year, so that no additional appropriations are required.

The commerce of the United States, and with it the navigating interests, have steadily and rapidly increased since the organization of our Government, until, it is believed, we are now second to but one power in the world, and at no distant day we shall probably be inferior to none. Exposed as they must be, it has been a wise policy to afford to these important interests protection with our ships of war distributed in the great highways of trade throughout the world. For more than thirty years appropriations have been made and annually expended for the gradual increase of our naval forces. In peace our Navy performs the important duty of protecting our commerce, and in the event of war will be, as it has been, a most efficient means of defense.

The successful use of steam navigation on the ocean has been followed by the introduction of war steamers in great and increasing numbers into the navies of the principal maritime powers of the world. A due regard to our own safety and to an efficient protection to our large and increasing commerce demands a corresponding increase on our part. No country has greater facilities for the construction of vessels of this description than ours, or can promise itself greater advantages from their employment. They are admirably adapted to the protection of our commerce, to the rapid transmission of intelligence, and to the coast defense. In pursuahce of the wise policy of a gradual increase of our Navy, large supplies of live-oak timber and other materials for shipbuilding have been collected and are now under shelter and in a state of good preservation, while iron steamers can be built with great facility in various parts of the Union. The use of iron as a material, especially in the construction of steamers which can enter with safety many of the harbors along our coast now inaccessible to vessels of greater draft, and the practicability of constructing them in the interior, strongly recommend that liberal appropriations should be made for this important object. Whatever may have been our policy in the earlier stages of the Government, when the nation was in its infancy, our shipping interests and commerce comparatively small, our resources limited, our population sparse and scarcely extending beyond the limits of the original thirteen States, that policy must be essentially different now that we have grown from three to more than twenty millions of people, that our commerce, carried in our own ships, is found in every sea, and that our territorial boundaries and settlements have been so greatly expanded. Neither our commerce nor our long line of coast on the ocean and on the Lakes can be successfully defended against foreign aggression by means of fortifications alone. These are essential at important commercial and military points, but our chief reliance for this object must be on a well-organized, efficient navy. The benefits resulting from such a navy are not confined to the Atlantic States. The productions of the interior which seek a market abroad are directly dependent on the safety and freedom of our commerce. The occupation of the Balize below New Orleans by a hostile force would embarrass, if not stagnate, the whole export trade of the Mississippi and affect the value of the agricultural products of the entire valley of that mighty river and its tributaries.

It has never been our policy to maintain large standing armies in time of peace. They are contrary to the genius of our free institutions, would impose heavy burdens on the people and be dangerous to public liberty. Our reliance for protection and defense on the land must be mainly on our citizen soldiers, who will be ever ready, as they ever have been ready in times past, to rush with alacrity, at the call of their country, to her defense. This description of force, however, can not defend our coast, harbors, and inland seas, nor protect our commerce on the ocean or the Lakes. These must be protected by our Navy.

Considering an increased naval force, and especially of steam vessels, corresponding with our growth and importance as a nation, and proportioned to the increased and increasing naval power of other nations, of vast importance as regards our safety, and the great and growing interests to be protected by it, I recommend the subject to the favorable consideration of Congress.

The report of the Postmaster-General herewith communicated contains a detailed statement of the operations of his Department during the pass year. It will be seen that the income from postages will fall short of the expenditures for the year between $1,000,000 and $2,000,000. This deficiency has been caused by the reduction of the rates of postage, which was made by the act of the 3d of March last. No principle has been more generally acquiesced in by the people than that this Department should sustain itself by limiting its expenditures to its income. Congress has never sought to make it a source of revenue for general purposes except for a short period during the last war with Great Britain, nor should it ever become a charge on the general Treasury. If Congress shall adhere to this principle, as I think they ought, it will be necessary either to curtail the present mail service so as to reduce the expenditures, or so to modify the act of the 3d of March last as to improve its revenues. The extension of the mail service and the additional facilities which will be demanded by the rapid extension and increase of population on our western frontier will not admit of such curtailment as will materially reduce the present expenditures. In the adjustment of the tariff of postages the interests of the people demand that the lowest rates be adopted which will produce the necessary revenue to meet the expenditures of the Department. I invite the attention of Congress to the suggestions of the Postmaster-General on this subject, under the belief that such a modification of the late law may be made as will yield sufficient revenue without further calls on the Treasury, and with very little change in the present rates of postage. Proper measures have been taken in pursuance of the act of the 3d of March last for the establishment of lines of mail steamers between this and foreign countries. The importance of this service commends itself strongly to favorable consideration.

With the growth of our country the public business which devolves on the heads of the several Executive Departments has greatly increased. In some respects the distribution of duties among them seems to be incongruous, and many of these might be transferred from one to another with advantage to the public interests. A more auspicious time for the consideration of this subject by Congress, with a view to system in the organization of the several Departments and a more appropriate division of the public business, will not probably occur.

The most important duties of the State Department relate to our foreign affairs. By the great enlargement of the family of nations, the increase of our commerce, and the corresponding extension of our consular system the business of this Department has been greatly increased. In its present organization many duties of a domestic nature and consisting of details are devolved on the Secretary of State, which do not appropriately belong to the foreign department of the Government and may properly be transferred to some other Department. One of these grows out of the present state of the law concerning the Patent Office, which a few years since was a subordinate clerkship, but has become a distinct bureau of great importance. With an excellent internal organization, it is still connected with the State Department. In the transaction of its business questions of much importance to inventors and to the community frequently arise, which by existing laws are referred for decision to a board of which the Secretary of State is a member. These questions are legal, and the connection which now exists between the State Department and the Patent Office may with great propriety and advantage be transferred to the Attorney-General.

In his last annual message to Congress Mr. Madison invited attention to a proper provision for the Attorney-General as "an important improvement in the executive establishment." This recommendation was repeated by some of his successors. The official duties of the Attorney-General have been much increased within a few years, and his office has become one of great importance. His duties may be still further increased with advantage to the public interests. As an executive officer his residence and constant attention at the seat of Government are required. Legal questions involving important principles and large amounts of public money are constantly referred to him by the President and Executive Departments for his examination and decision. The public business under his official management before the judiciary has been so augmented by the extension of our territory and the acts of Congress authorizing suits against the United States for large bodies of valuable public lands as greatly to increase his labors and responsibilities. I therefore recommend that the Attorney-General be placed on the same footing with the heads of the other Executive Departments, with such subordinate officers provided by law for his Department as may be required to discharge the additional duties which have been or may be devolved upon him.

Congress possess the power of exclusive legislation over the District of Columbia, and I commend the interests of its inhabitants to your favorable consideration. The people of this District have no legislative body of their own, and must confide their local as well as their general interests to representatives in whose election they have no voice and over whose official conduct they have no control. Each member of the National Legislature should consider himself as their immediate representative, and should be the more ready to give attention to their interests and wants because he is not responsible to them. I recommend that a liberal and generous spirit may characterize your measures in relation to them. I shall be ever disposed to show a proper regard for their wishes and, within constitutional limits, shall at all times cheerfully cooperate with you for the advancement of their welfare.

I trust it may not be deemed inappropriate to the occasion for me to dwell for a moment on the memory of the most eminent citizen of our country who during the summer that is gone by has descended to the tomb. The enjoyment of contemplating, at the advanced age of near fourscore years, the happy condition of his country cheered the last hours of Andrew Jackson, who departed this life in the tranquil hope of a blessed immortality. His death was happy, as his life had been eminently useful. He had an unfaltering confidence in the virtue and capacity of the people and in the permanence of that free Government which he had largely contributed to establish and defend. His great deeds had secured to him the affections of his fellow-citizens, and it was his happiness to witness the growth and glory of his country, which he loved so well. He departed amidst the benedictions of millions of free-men. The nation paid its tribute to his memory at his tomb. Coming generations will learn from his example the love of country and the rights of man. In his language on a similar occasion to the present, "I now commend you, fellow-citizens, to the guidance of Almighty God, with a full reliance on His merciful providence for the maintenance of our free institutions, and with an earnest supplication that whatever errors it may be my lot to commit in discharging the arduous duties which have devolved on me will find a remedy in the harmony and wisdom of your counsels."